I WILL LIFT UP MINE EYES
UNTO THE HILLS
FROM WHENCE
COMETH MY
STRENGTH

THE
CUMBERLAND
WAY

HILLSIDE GUIDES

LONG DISTANCE WALKS
- 1 • THE WESTMORLAND WAY
- 2 • THE FURNESS WAY
- 3 • THE CUMBERLAND WAY
- 7 • CLEVELAND WAY COMPANION
- 9 • THE NORTH BOWLAND TRAVERSE
  (by David Johnson)
- 16 • DALES WAY COMPANION
- 22 • THE COAST TO COAST WALK

CIRCULAR WALKS – YORKSHIRE DALES
- 4 • WALKS IN WHARFEDALE
- 5 • WALKS IN NIDDERDALE
- 6 • WALKS IN THE CRAVEN DALES
- 8 • WALKS IN WENSLEYDALE
- 10 • WALKS IN THREE PEAKS COUNTRY
- 11 • WALKS IN SWALEDALE
- 20 • RAMBLES IN WHARFEDALE
- 21 • WALKS ON THE HOWGILL FELLS

CIRCULAR WALKS – NORTH YORK MOORS
- 13 • WESTERN – Cleveland/Hambleton Hills
- 14 • SOUTHERN – Rosedale/Farndale/Bransdale
- 15 • NORTHERN – Eskdale and the Coast

CIRCULAR WALKS – SOUTH PENNINES
- 12 • WALKS IN BRONTE COUNTRY
- 17 • WALKS IN CALDERDALE

HILLWALKING – LAKE DISTRICT
- 18 • OVER LAKELAND MOUNTAINS
- 19 • OVER LAKELAND FELLS

FREEDOM OF THE DALES
40 selected walks
Full colour hardback

---

80 DALES WALKS
Omnibus edition of Books 4,6,8,11 and (in part)10,21
Published by Cordee, Leicester

THE
CUMBERLAND
WAY

by

Paul Hannon

HILLSIDE  PUBLICATIONS

HILLSIDE PUBLICATIONS
11 Nessfield Grove
Exley Head
Keighley
West Yorkshire
BD22 6NU

First published 1985
Revised edition 1990
3rd impression 1993

FOR SANDRA

Who in the midst of preparing
for our first born gave unstinting support
to enable this work to be completed

Illustrations

Page 1: Church window, Wasdale Head
Page 6: Cumberland coat of arms

The maps in this book are based upon the
1900 - 1920 Ordnance Survey 1:10,560 (6") maps

ISBN 1 870141 11 3

Printed in Great Britain by
Caranmor Print and Design
95/97 London Road
Preston
Lancashire
PR1 4BA

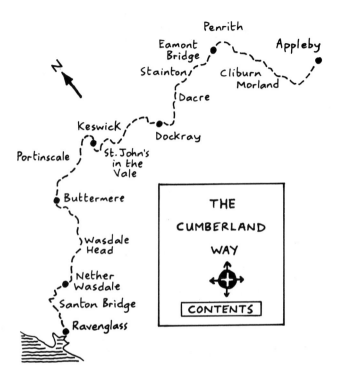

Introduction	6
The Route Guide	11
Ravenglass to Nether Wasdale	12
Nether Wasdale to Buttermere	20
Buttermere to Keswick	30
Keswick to Dockray	40
Dockray to Eamont Bridge	50
Eamont Bridge to Appleby	66
A log of the walk	80
Index	86

INTRODUCTION

In 1974 the county of Cumberland went the way of its two smaller neighbours, Westmorland and Lancashire 'north of the sands', and their combined demise created the all-embracing Cumbria. A small corner of the West Riding of Yorkshire was even added for good measure. Although the new county does possess an inspiring and historic name, it fails to stir the imagination in quite the same way.

In boyhood the name Cumberland conjured up visions of sweeping mountains and deep blue lakes, and it is these very mountains and lakes that form the heart of the Cumberland Way. The walk stretches from Ravenglass on the coast, across the National Park section of the county to the Westmorland boundary, to end in that county at Appleby. It will easily be deduced that the Way links, through the shared termini of Appleby, Arnside and Ravenglass, with the Westmorland Way and the Furness Way. As such, sections of any could be amalgamated, even going as far as combining all three in their entirety to form a memorable 250-mile circular exploration of this wonderful county.

The 80 miles of the Cumberland Way fit comfortably into a week, with an average of 13 miles walking over six days. The guide has been divided into that many sections, each describing a day that ends with or near suitable accommodation. By far the shortest days are the

At Wanthwaite

6

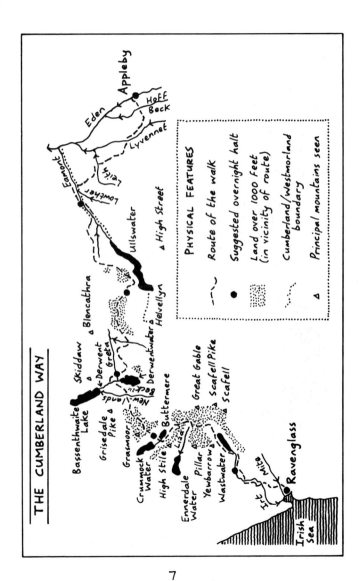

THE CUMBERLAND WAY

PHYSICAL FEATURES

Route of the walk — ·· —
Suggested overnight halt ●
Land over 1000 Feet (in vicinity of route)
Cumberland/Westmorland boundary
Principal mountains seen ▲

Appleby
Eden
Hoff Beck
Lyvennet
Eamont
Lowther
A1247
High Street ▲
Ullswater
Helvellyn ▲
Skiddaw ▲ Blencathra ▲
Derwent Greta
Grisedale Pike ▲ Derwentwater
Bassenthwaite Lake
Newlands
Grasmoor ▲
Crummock Water
High Stile ▲ Buttermere
Ennerdale Water
Pillar ▲
Yewbarrow ▲
Great Gable ▲
Scafell Pike ▲
Scafell ▲
Wastwater
Irt
Mite
Ravenglass
Irish Sea

first and third, the first to allow for late starts and unprepared limbs, the other permitting an alternative ridge walk or a potter round Keswick and Derwentwater.

At first glance it may appear odd that the Way does not take in any mountain summits, preferring as it does to seek out the passes and old tracks through the hills. The advantage of this is that rough weather that might put the tops out of bounds need not hamper the walk: the route is virtually infallible where it crosses the fells, and it is better to use the Way as a springboard to loftier fare if opportunities should arise. A glance at the 1" Tourist map will reveal the wealth of options in the fell country between Wasdale and Gowbarrow. One or two of these are mentioned at the relevant stage in the text.

Each suggested overnight halt provides accommodation of some kind, though not all can match the choice at Keswick and Appleby. Youth hostels, B+B's and hotels are reasonably well spread, as are campsites for the more adventurous. Two less well served spots are Dockray and Eamont Bridge: the former is only a mile from Ullswater with its own bus service linking Penrith and Patterdale, while the latter is virtually on the outskirts of all-welcoming Penrith. Probably the best guide to B+B accommodation covering the whole area is the annually published yearbook of the Ramblers' Association.

Both terminal points of the walk are served by public transport, and in each case it is the railway that provides the more practical service.

EARLY CLOSING / MARKET DAYS

	Early closing	Market
Keswick	Wed.	Sat.
Penrith	Wed.	Tue/Sat.
Appleby	Thur.	Sat.

At Santon Bridge

SOME USEFUL FACILITIES
This is a general guide ONLY

	YHA	other accom.	inn	bus service	railway	post office	other shop	WC	payphone
Ravenglass		✓	✓	✓	✓	✓	✓		✓
Santon Bridge		✓	✓			✓			✓
Nether Wasdale	✓	✓	✓						✓
Wasdale Head		✓	✓				✓	✓	✓
Black Sail Hut	✓								
Buttermere	✓	✓	✓	✓			✓	✓	✓
Portinscale		✓	✓	✓		✓	✓		✓
Crosthwaite		✓	✓	✓					
Keswick	✓	✓	✓	✓		✓	✓	✓	✓
Vale of St. John		✓							✓
Dockray		✓	✓	✓		✓			✓
Aira Force				✓			✓	✓	
Dacre		✓	✓			✓			✓
Stainton		✓	✓			✓			✓
Yanwath		✓	✓						✓
Eamont Bridge		✓	✓	✓	Penrith	✓			✓
Cliburn		✓	✓						✓
Morland		✓	✓			✓			✓
King's Meaburn			✓			✓			✓
Appleby		✓	✓	✓	✓	✓	✓	✓	✓

ORDNANCE SURVEY MAPS REQUIRED

These excellent maps complement the strip-maps in the guide by giving an overall picture of the countryside encountered, and showing the off-route features which may be of use or interest.

1:50,000 Landranger: 89,96 (tiny portions); 90, 91 or, only sheet 91 with the 1" Tourist Map

Because of the guide's detailed strip-maps, the above are probably more advantageous than 2½" (1:25,000) maps, of which five would be required.

Outdoor Leisure: 4, 5, 6 (English Lakes NW, NE, SW)
Pathfinder: 578: Appleby in Westmorland
          597: Crosby Ravensworth + Brough

SOME USEFUL ADDRESSES

The Ramblers' Association
 1/5 Wandsworth Rd, London SW8 2XX
    Tel. 071-582 6878

Youth Hostels Association
 Trevelyan House, St. Albans, Herts AL1 2DY
    Tel. 0727-55215

Lake District National Park Visitors Services
 Brockhole, Windermere LA23 1LJ
    Tel. 05394-46601

Cumbria Tourist Board
 Ashleigh, Holly Road, Windermere LA23 2AQ
    Tel. 05394-44444

The National Trust
 Regional Office: Rothay Holme, Ambleside LA22 0EJ
    Tel. 05394-33883

Friends of the Lake District
 No.3, Yard 77, Highgate, Kendal LA9 4ED
    Tel. 0539-720788
    (NOT an information service)

Cumberland Motor Services
 Tangier Street, Whitehaven
    Tel. 0946-63222
 Brunswick Road, Penrith
    Tel. 0768-63616

Mountain Goat Minibus Company
 Victoria Street, Windermere
    Tel. 05394-45161

Lake District Weather Forecast 05394-45151

Tourist Information
      Ravenglass   06577-278
      Gosforth   0900-2923
      Keswick   0596-72645
      Penrith   0768-64671
      Appleby   0930-51177

THE ROUTE GUIDE

The bulk of this book is a detailed guide to the walk itself, extending from page 12 to page 79. It is divided into six daily sections, each of which has its own introduction: these can be located most easily by reference to the contents on page 5.

A continuous strip-map runs throughout the guide, accompanied by a narrative of the route on the same or facing page. The remainder of each page is then given over to notes and illustrations of the many places of interest along the way.

The maps are at the scale of 2½ inches to one mile, and the top of the page is always North.

Key to the map symbols

Route   _ _ _ clear _ _ _   sketchy   no path

Route on public road   wall   unenclosed   Fence/hedge

Abbreviations   g = gate   Railway line
s = stile   c = cattle grid

Buildings   Church   Cairns   summit   other

Crags   Loose rock /scree   Marsh   Trees

river or beck   tarn or lake   bridge   waterfall

Miles from Ravenglass   (73)

Map continuation (indicates page number)   39

SECTION 1

—— RAVENGLASS TO NETHER WASDALE ——

9½ miles   350 feet of ascent

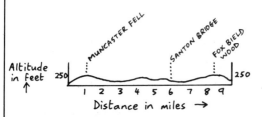

Altitude in feet ↑

MUNCASTER FELL

SANTON BRIDGE

FOX FIELD WOOD

250   250

1 2 3 4 5 6 7 8 9

Distance in miles →

A nice easy start to set the ball rolling, with the coastline being vacated almost immediately. The Ravenglass and Eskdale Railway is met at restored Muncaster Mill, with farm roads leading to isolated Irton Church and its Anglian cross. After a close encounter with Irton Hall, Santon Bridge is reached. From the hamlet paths alongside or near the river Irt guide steps to Nether Wasdale.

Ravenglass

Ravenglass

Sheltering in its own little haven on the Cumbrian coast, Ravenglass forms a start to the walk which is far removed from the mountainous country to be encountered in the days ahead. The village's shelter is created by the natural indentations of the coastline which protect it from the worst excesses of the weather. Mainly in the form of dunes, land reaches out a mile further in the shape of the two outer arms of the rivers Irt and Esk. Immediately in front of Ravenglass they join forces with the Mite, striking out to the sea collectively as the Esk. A nature reserve exists on the dunes, which offer an ideal habitat for the flora and fauna that can cope with above average radiation.

The village itself consists of little more than a main street and the environs of the Ravenglass + Eskdale Railway, which has its headquarters here. Indeed, were it not for the railway, then this would be a veritable ghost town. As it is, one's opening steps along the street to the beach might seem curiously reminiscent of a scene from 'High Noon'. The solitude of Ravenglass has much to do with its inaccessibility, as well as its proximity to Windscale: the majority of motorists must cross the Lake District to get here, and most are waylaid by something else well before their winding road brings them to the coast.

Many centuries ago Ravenglass was an important port, used by the Romans. They built a fort here- Glannoventa- on which now stands Walls Mansion. Of most interest now are the remains known as Walls Castle, pictured → The Romans' bath house, it is said to be the tallest remaining example of the Romans' domesticity in the country.

A mile to the east stands Muncaster Castle, a big house in beautiful grounds. The richly coloured walls include a pele tower, and augmented by various additions it is open to view, courtesy of the centuries-old occupants, the Pennington's.

The Route

A journey of a thousand miles begins with the first step, and the first step from Ravenglass is a bizarre one indeed, leaving the main street at it's southern extremity where it abruptly terminates on the beach. Staying close to the more solid ground, bear left and leave the shore at the very first little inlet, along an enclosed path to pass under the railway line and emerge onto the drive to Walls Mansion.✱NB: If the tide should be fully in, it might be necessary to join the drive by a footpath by the side of the hotel, leading to a footbridge over the railway and keeping on to reach the drive at its junction with the road.

Where the main route meets the drive, go straight over to a stile and keep on to a wicket gate. Now head diagonally across a vast field, using a lone gatepost for the required direction. A wicket gate admits to woodland, through which a good path climbs to the main road. Go left for 150 yards then take a broad track on the right. After leaving the trees behind this splendid track crosses down-like terrain, giving excellent views of Ravenglass in its grip of sand dunes.

After intervening fences the track forks above a solitary house. The most direct route is the left branch, a permissive path that saves climbing and doubling back. It emerges at a junction of paths behind Muncaster Mill: drop down to pass between the buildings and out along its drive onto the main road. Turn right over railway and river bridges, then as the road gently climbs, take the first farm track on the right. It heads Roman fashion for Gasketh, with the Wasdale fells drawing us ever closer.

Muncaster Mill —

a renovated cornmill whose waterwheel now turns again to help produce flour for purchase by visitors. A small fee is payable for a proper look round the mill.

The Ravenglass and Eskdale Railway was opened in 1875 to transport iron ore from the mines in Eskdale to the main line at Ravenglass. In no time at all it was also carrying passengers. From the demise of that venture to its acquisition by a preservation society in the 1960s it had a chequered history, being opened and closed numerous times and almost disappearing completely.

Today it is a very successful concern, and thousands travel on 'La'al Ratty's narrow gauge line every year, more often than not behind a steam engine.

An overlap with the Furness Way occurs for five minutes only, as far as the drive through the plantation.

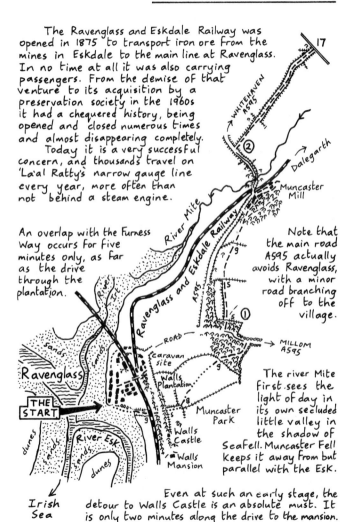

Note that the main road A595 actually avoids Ravenglass, with a minor road branching off to the village.

The river Mite first sees the light of day in its own secluded little valley in the shadow of Seafell. Muncaster Fell keeps it away from but parallel with the Esk.

Even at such an early stage, the detour to Walls Castle is an absolute must. It is only two minutes along the drive to the mansion.

15

On arriving at the junction of farm roads at Gasketh turn left along another broad track between hedges. Eventually the unswerving Holmrook-Eskdale Green road is crossed straight over, a long drive, initially surfaced, rising past the former school and rectory on what becomes an idyllic byway to Irton Church. After a potter about, take the wicket gate on the right as the car park was entered, and head directly away alongside a fence.

Beyond an intervening stile a natural groove is followed above a wood, and from the fence where it ends aim across the field to the far corner. Continue away with a fence to pass through a breach in the narrow strip of woodland ahead. Once through the gap follow another fence away: when it bears away to the left keep straight on, across a large tract of parkland towards a gate with greenhouses in the grounds of Irton Hall behind.

Without entering the grounds turn right with the fence, clinging to it when it bends left to arrive at a stile into the grounds. A short green way runs along to join a drive with houses to the left and the hall itself across a large lawn on the left. Turn right along the drive to emerge onto a lane adjacent to the former lodge. Go left along the narrow lane for a long half-mile, and after it has swung right for a steep but short climb, locate an iron kissing gate on the left. From it a path descends through trees to a gate by the Irt. A very brief stroll alongside the river is curtailed by Santon Bridge. From a wall-stile go left on the road over the bridge.

Santon Bridge

16

The parish church of St. Paul, Irton dates from the 19th century, and though its immediate predecessor lasted only sixty years, churches have occupied the site for over a thousand years. The only visible reminder is a very special one: a 9th century Anglian cross, a tall block of sandstone with excellently preserved carvings. Note also the attractive lych-gate and war memorial.

Santon Bridge

River Irt

19

ESKDALE GREEN

Santon Bridge is barely even a hamlet, consisting of an inn, tiny Post office, and several farms and cottages all scattered on or near the banks of the river.

Irton Church ④

Irton Hall ⑤

ESKDALE GREEN

The river Irt has a glorious start, emerging from Wastwater in the shadow of the majestic Screes. As we soon discover, its course is a very circuitous one.

HOLMROOK ← ESKDALE GREEN → SANTONBRIDGE

Originally a 14th century pele tower and long-time home of the Irton family, and since a school, the hall has now been converted to modern apartments.

Muncaster Fell overlooks Gasketh

Anglian Cross, Irton Church

Moorgate ③

Gasketh

15

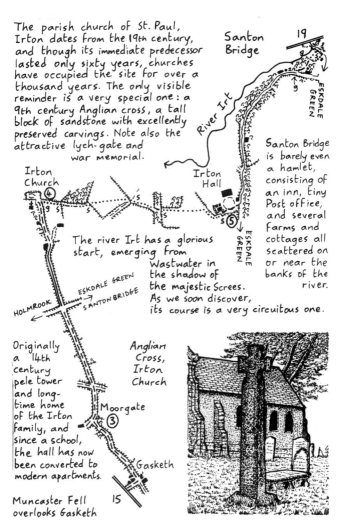

The Route

Having crossed the bridge to the inn, leave the road just before it on a broad track heading up-river. A bend in the Irt is given the short-cut treatment in the company of a mill race, and shortly afterwards the drive is vacated in order to keep faith with the riverbank. This is now followed tightly round several bends in the most tranquil of surroundings. Sometimes with a path, sometimes without, the riverbank leads unerringly to Craghouse Bridge.

Do not cross the bridge, but head left up a lane to leave it almost at once along a surfaced drive going off to the right. It crosses the river by means of Hollins Bridge, a shapely arch with a pipe-bearing twin. Heading away from the river the drive rises to Hollins Farm. At the entrance to the yard take a stile on the left to use an oft-muddy track which loses itself in a large field. Aim for a prominent knoll, deflecting round to its left to arrive at a gate in the corner behind.

A walled track is entered and followed along to the left. When the woods end turn sharp right on a good track which leads, again unerringly, to the farmstead of Stangends. Do not enter its confines but bear left over the field and down to a gate. From it a track enters the wooded environs of the river Irt once more. Cross the bridge in front and head directly away with the wall, to pass through a gate into the corner of Birks Wood.

A good path runs through the trees and rises steadily to leave by a gateway, then bears right across a field to locate a wicket gate. A gem of a green lane is joined, and followed all too briefly to the right to emerge in Nether Wasdale.

Craghouse
Bridge

The scattered little village of Nether Wasdale is spread along a wide section of minor road, suggesting that its alternative name of Strands is as equally appropriate as this geographically sound version. Focal point is where the two whitewashed inns glare at each other across the street, with the attractive little church nestling in trees only a few yards distant.

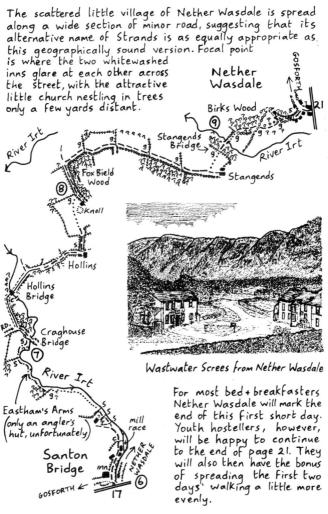

Wastwater Screes from Nether Wasdale

For most bed + breakfasters Nether Wasdale will mark the end of this first short day. Youth hostellers, however, will be happy to continue to the end of page 21. They will also then have the bonus of spreading the first two days' walking a little more evenly.

19

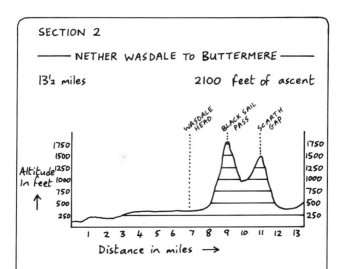

SECTION 2

—— NETHER WASDALE TO BUTTERMERE ——

13½ miles   2100 feet of ascent

Altitude
In feet

Distance in miles →

This second day is almost entirely enclosed in rugged fells. Three valleys are taken in, and the company of two splendid lakes enjoyed. The length of Wastwater and the hallowed climbing centre of Wasdale Head precede a climb through Black Sail Pass into lonely Ennerdale. Scarth Gap Pass is the gateway to the Buttermere valley, amidst breathtaking mountain scenery.

Yewbarrow
from
Wastwater

The Route

From the two hotels in the village head east on the Wasdale road to reach an open triangle where three roads meet. Bear right over both bridges and onto the Santon Bridge road. Leave it immediately, however, by a gate on the left, and follow the long farm road all the way to Easthwaite.

Head straight through the centre of this lively farmstead - more of a hamlet - and leave it by a clear track at the far end. At a fork it bears left through a gate, shortly to become confined for a brief spell. On emerging into a field corner, vacate the track and turn left down the field-side to a wicket gate at the bottom. Go left again the few yards to cross the river Irt and Lund Bridge, which is the first crossing of Wastwater's outflow.

Turn right over the bridge, with a National Trust sign indicating a permissive path. As Low Wood is entered all becomes plain sailing, and attention can be devoted to the delightful surroundings. This excellent path follows first the river and in turn the shore of Wastwater, which soon opens out to provide a foreground to spectacular mountain scenery. When Wasdale Hall appears the path leaves the wood but remains by the lake, to return to woodland beyond the hostel.

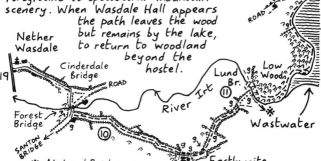

※ At Lund Bridge an alternative route to the head of the lake presents itself. This traverse of the southern shore of Wastwater enjoys a spectacular intimacy with the famous Screes, but in its early stages is EXCESSIVELY arduous.

21

Wasdale Hall

A youth hostel since the early 1970s, the striking hall has retained its fine interior, dominated by some splendidly carved oak features.

The Route

The path continues along the shoreline, until the last stile takes it out of the grounds and up onto the road. Exactly at this point the road emerges from its confines into the unshackled glory of Echo Corner, with the length of Wastwater stretching away into the mountain fastnesses of the dalehead. This narrow strip of tarmac, with softer verges much of the way, is our route for the next 3 miles, and must be the most spectacular road-walk in England.

Half a mile past the head of the lake, the road goes right over an arched bridge, and can now be vacated to gain Wasdale Head by the path along the left side of the beck. It runs to a pack bridge to double back into the hamlet.

Lingmell, Scafell Pike and Scafell from Wastwater

The magnificently sited sheep farm of Bowderdale also has famous fell-running connections

Wastwater is a wonderful sheet of water, descriptions of which inevitably ooze superlatives. A mere three miles in length, and lacking any great shape, it is nevertheless the deepest lake in England, reaching a maximum of 257 feet. Wastwater's mood can change more rapidly than the tamer lakes, with much depending on the mountains rising behind, from the classic view up to Wasdale Head to the unforgettable backdrop of the Screes.

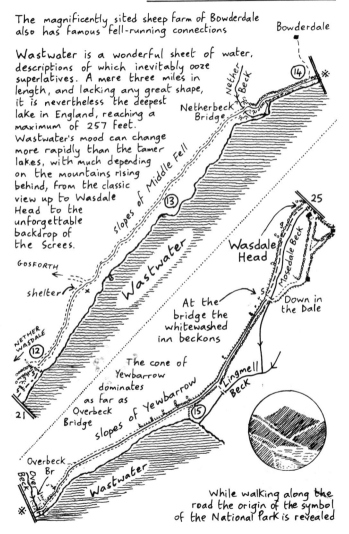

Bowderdale

Nether Beck

Netherbeck Bridge

slopes of Middle Fell

⑭

⑬

Wastwater

25

Wasdale Head

Mosedale Beck

Down in the Dale

At the bridge the whitewashed inn beckons

GOSFORTH

shelter ✕

NETHER WASDALE

⑫

21

The cone of Yewbarrow dominates as far as Overbeck Bridge

slopes of Yewbarrow

slopes of Yewbarrow

Lingmell Beck

⑮

Overbeck Br

Over Beck

✻

Wastwater

While walking along the road the origin of the symbol of the National Park is revealed

The Route

As Wasdale Head is so claustrophobically crowded by mountains, it should come as no surprise that our route makes its escape through the fells. From the inn return to the beckside and the packhorse bridge just upstream. Do not cross it however, but accompany the beck upstream on a wide track. A short rise to a gate then admits to the open fellside, and the well worn path to the left should be taken beneath the steep slopes of Kirk Fell.

This pleasant path remains surprisingly level for a good while yet, passing through a small gate to approach the magnificent amphitheatre of the head of Mosedale. For a time there is apparently no easy escape, but at an immense cairn the main path bears right and soon begins to climb in earnest. Gatherstone Beck is crossed by any of a hundred natural stepping stones, and the old pony track curves across the fellside before a final pull onto the top of Black Sail Pass. As the going eases to reach the cairn, a well earned rest can be enjoyed in the heart of the mountains.

Pillar from Row Head packhorse bridge, Wasdale Head

The zigzags above the crossing of Gatherstone Beck are far more favourable than the steep grind which cuts through them. But then zigzags always are.

From the pass Kirkfell Crags appear rather intimidating, while the path up the Pillar ridge looks positively inviting

Black Sail Pass   27

1800'

18

Gatherstone Beck

Kirkfell Crags

17

Mosedale Beck

slopes of Kirk Fell

16   Wasdale Head

23

Opportunity to lighten one's load is available alongside Mosedale Beck, where a National Trust collection box can relieve one of any loose change acquired in the hotel bar.

Wasdale Head is a mecca for fellwalkers and climbers, steeped in tradition as a home of British rock climbing. It is not difficult to see why, encircled as it is by some of England's finest mountains, from Pillar and Great Gable to the Scafell group. The hamlet stands at the head of a cul de sac, its remoteness to motorists being a positive boon to walkers. Paths radiate through the hills to Ennerdale, Borrowdale, Eskdale and further afield. From here, Seathwaite in Borrowdale is only 5 miles by foot, yet the motorist will clock up more than 40 miles getting there. Despite its fame, Wasdale Head is a tiny farming community with a famous hostelry and a tiny church (St. Olaf's) hidden in trees in the corner of a field: several of its gravestones tell the same sad tale. In contrast, the whitewashed hotel is a veritable beacon to walkers on the fells high above. Adjacent to it is a barn-shop

The Route

A long redundant but still operational gate on the summit of the pass caters for the short-sighted, and from it the track begins a steep descent into the head of Ennerdale. The narrow footbridge over the river Liza is reached in no time at all, the height lost being a mere 900 feet. On crossing the bridge turn left down the valley, the wide path skirting the upper limit of the forest and soon reaching Black Sail Hut.

Continue down the valley on the hut's broad access track, but when it enters the dark confines of the forest leave it in favour of the path climbing to the right. Skirting the boundary of the plantation, the path soon rises above the trees and continues climbing to soon gain the tilted crest of Scarth Gap Pass. Once again a deserved rest can be enjoyed, happy in the knowledge that on this occasion the day's climbing has ceased.

As with the preceding Black Sail Pass, the start of the descent is an immediate one, on a very popular path with superlative views.

The Gables from Black Sail Hut

Scarth Gap is one of the district's less demanding passes, connecting the Buttermere and Ennerdale valleys. From its crest at 1485 feet, a magnificent ridgewalk sets off to the west along the summits of the High Stile group, while to the east the ground rises sharply to rugged Haystacks, probably the Lake District's grandest sub-2000 foot Fell. The sudden view from the top of the pass of Buttermere and the Grasmoor Fells is one of the highlights of the Cumberland Way.

Ennerdale has always been a quiet valley, and for many years now its steep slopes have held a deeper loneliness, compliments of the Forestry Commission. The appeal of such a bleak landscape is surely in its natural state, not man's idea of improvement. The Liza loses its identity in Ennerdale Water down the valley.

Black Sail is a classic mountain pass squeezing between imposing peaks of astonishing grandeur. Though connecting the heads of Ennerdale and Wasdale it is seldom used solely as such, but more often as either a stepping stone to the summits, or in league with Scarth Gap to reach Buttermere, exactly as we are intending to do.

Not unexpectedly, Black Sail Hut is Lakeland's most isolated youth hostel. This former shepherd's hut is also probably the most dramatically sited in the country. Its atmosphere is unsurpassed.

29

20
Scarth
Seat   Gap
Haystacks

Black Sail
Hut
19

Ennerdale Forest

River Liza

Sail Beck

25

27

Buttermere is the tiniest of villages, with an equally tiny church, and two large hotels which dominate the centre of the place. The excellent youth hostel is found just out on the Honister road, and was itself a hotel at one time. Buttermere village stands near to the head of the valley of the same name, adjacent to the short, green strath which separates the waters of Crummock and Buttermere.

The valley is a real gem, unquestionably one of Lakeland's finest. Here the mountains rise particularly steeply all round, the only easy escape being along the road which squeezes between Crummock Water and the Grasmoor fells to reach the Vale of Lorton. Two motor roads negotiate exciting passes to reach neighbouring dales. The Newlands Pass (sometimes referred to as Buttermere Hause) is the direct route to Keswick by way of the Newlands valley, while the more widely used Honister Pass climbs out of the valley head under the imposing Honister Crag to reach Borrowdale. These two combined to form the 'Buttermere round', a popular coach-and-four excursion from Keswick in days gone by.

Today, in spite of its ravishing beauty, the village is still not over-run with tourists, the happy failure of it to expand, and the resulting lack of gift shops proving to have been its saviour.

Fleetwith Pike from the foot of Buttermere

The Route

As the head of Buttermere is reached, a zig-zag path descends steeply to the right: ignore it and keep left as the path eases out to follow the lakeshore. After Comb Beck the path forks: take the right branch which enters Burtness Wood almost by the lakeside.

This National Trust path remains close to the water all the way to the foot of the lake, joining a wider track part way. After two neighbouring bridges the track heads directly for the village.

The lakeside walk, with its fine views over the water to the Grasmoor group of fells rising behind the village, makes for a perfect end to the day.

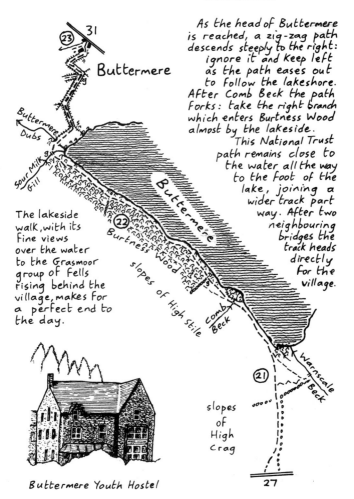

Buttermere Youth Hostel

SECTION 3

─── BUTTERMERE TO KESWICK ───

10 miles   1600 feet of ascent

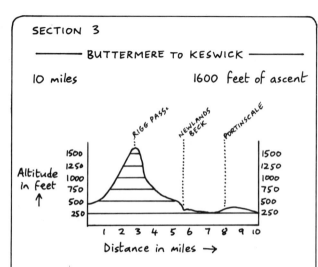

The Buttermere valley is left by a superb footpath that climbs gently through imposing mountains to emerge into the verdant Newlands valley. The shapely Grasmoor and Newlands Fells dominate the day as the Way uses field and woodland paths to reach Portinscale. From this tiny village the outstanding church at Crosthwaite precedes a quiet entry into the bustle of Keswick.

Haystacks from across Scarth Gap — near the end of Section 2

The Route

To leave Buttermere cross the road bridge in front of the aptly named hotel and take a wicket gate on the right. A good path heads up through the trees above Sail Beck, climbing even higher after a left fork to arrive at a solid stile-cum-gate.

At once the open fellside is reached. Turn right along another good path, but after only a short distance opt for a path slanting gently off to the left just opposite where the adjacent wall returns to replace a short section of fence. This most enjoyable path rises so steadily across the fell that no effort at all is needed. Every step is a pleasure as the upper reaches of Sail Beck are penetrated.

Should the morning of departure from Buttermere be graced with first class weather, a splendid alternative exists in the form of a high level ridgewalk from Buttermere village to the foot of Rowling End. The small plan overleaf gives an idea of the route, though it goes without saying that a detailed map is essential.

With this third day being an easy one, this adventurous option doesn't really involve too much extra effort. In return one of the finest ridges in the district can be enjoyed, taking in no less than six individual tops: memorable stuff!

Addacomb Beck

32

slopes of Wandope

25

Third Gill

Sail Beck

slopes of Knott Rigg

24

slopes of Whiteless Pike

LORTON COCKERMOUTH B5289

Sail Beck

KESWICK

Buttermere

youth hostel

29

HONISTER PASS

BORROWDALE B5289

31

The Route

Having swung in to cross Addacomb Beck the path slopes across a short section of rough scree, though even here it remains well engineered. The fells now crowd in on the valley head, and the highest point of the pass is soon reached: a feeble cairn marks the spot. After a short, level hike the beginnings of Rigg Beck are crossed and the path starts to descend alongside.

Before long the path forks. Ignore the inviting trod to the left in favour of the rougher path remaining with the beck. One cannot possibly go astray from here on. After a rather steep drop through a large expanse of scree the path eases, and eventually the road is joined where it crosses the beck at a hairpin bend.

Turn left along the road from Rigg Beck as it clings to the tumbling slopes of Rowling End, and after a short half-mile take a gate on the right where a slate footpath sign points the way to Ghyll Bank and Skelgill. From it a path descends to cross the drive to Rowling End Farm, and from the gate across descends to a footbridge over Newlands Beck.

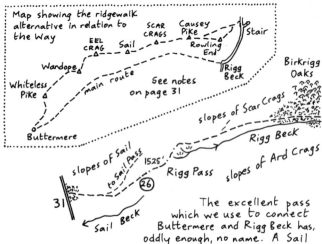

Map showing the ridgewalk alternative in relation to the Way

See notes on page 31

The excellent pass which we use to connect Buttermere and Rigg Beck has, oddly enough, no name. A Sail Pass already exists several hundred feet higher between Sail and Scar Crags and so the obvious suggestion of Rigg Pass is humbly offered by the author.

On the descent alongside Rigg Beck the rugged slopes of Ard Crags appear most impressive, but when the fell is seemingly out of one's mind, remember to cast a glance back. Only then, as the road is neared, does the shapely aspect depicted alongside appear.

Ard Crags
From
Rigg Beck

Again while with the beck, one cannot fail to notice the large cluster of windswept trees that cling to the 1200 – 1400 ft. contour. Known as the Birkrigg Oaks, this patch of sessile oak woodland is designated of special scientific interest due to its survival at a now unique altitude in this country. The distinction is shared with a larger group on Ard Crags' other flank.

The Newlands valley is one of Lakeland's most beautiful corners: with no lakes and no single honeypot for tourists it remains pleasantly unspoilt. Slaty mountains rise steeply on three sides, with the beck escaping north to the contrasting wide plain that precedes entry into Bassenthwaite Lake. The valley boasts a mining history in which lead and copper were won by Germans in the time of Elizabeth I. Today, all is harmoniously tranquil.

The house at Rigg Beck is unmistakable!

The Route

From the bridge over Newlands Beck head straight up the field to locate a small gate in the wall, just left of the farm buildings of Ghyll Bank. Turn left for a few yards along the narrow lane, then opt for another gate on the right. Head across the field to a stile, continuing up the next field to a stile at the top left, then swing round with the fence to a further stile. From it a lovely green track heads away to approach Skelgill.

A stile admits to the environs of this mini-hamlet, and after passing along the front of the first cottage, go right up the access road. Rising past the main buildings it passes through a gate to meet the open fell, then with all eyes on the view it runs along to meet the Grange-Portinscale road at the very foot of Catbells' north ridge.

Turn down the road in the midst of a series of sharp bends, but immediately after the cattle grid leave it by a wicket gate on the right: a green finger-post points the way to the Derwentwater launch pier. A well worn path drops down through the wood to a variety of signs at a meeting of lanes near Hawse End.

Take the advice of the sign pointing straight over the lane on the left. Through the wicket gate a popular path runs through a woodland tunnel towards Portinscale. It leaves the trees for a brief spell then returns with relish back into them, eventually emerging onto the drive to Lingholm.

Rowling End
and
Causey Pike
from Skelgill

*Looking back to
Hindscarth (2385')
Robinson (2417')
from above
Newlands Beck*

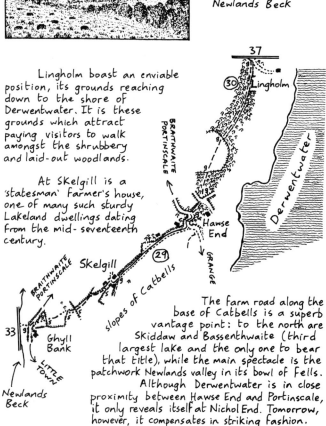

Lingholm boast an enviable
position, its grounds reaching
down to the shore of
Derwentwater. It is these
grounds which attract
paying visitors to walk
amongst the shrubbery
and laid-out woodlands.

At Skelgill is a
'statesman' farmer's house,
one of many such sturdy
Lakeland dwellings dating
from the mid-seventeenth
century.

The farm road along the
base of Catbells is a superb
vantage point: to the north are
Skiddaw and Bassenthwaite (third
largest lake and the only one to bear
that title), while the main spectacle is the
patchwork Newlands valley in its bowl of fells.
Although Derwentwater is in close
proximity between Hawse End and Portinscale,
it only reveals itself at Nichol End. Tomorrow,
however, it compensates in striking fashion.

35

The Route

From the gateway to Lingholm cross straight over the drive to a broad path heading away with a wall into the woods. As the wall swings away to the right, a more direct path through the trees of Fawe Park forges straight on, but the better option is to stay with the path by the wall. At the other end of Fawe Park's greenery a drive is met: crossing straight over the path drops down into the bustle of Nichol End landings on Derwentwater's shore. Go left along the lane to meet the Portinscale road only yards beyond the emergence of the aforementioned direct path.

Turn right for Portinscale and then right again in the village, passing a large hotel before coming to the road's abrupt demise. Fortunately pedestrians can continue, to cross a sizeable suspension bridge over the river Derwent, itself only just strengthened by the additional waters of Keswick's river, the Greta. At the opposite end of the footbridge the road resumes, running along to join the far more recently by-passed main road.

Our acquaintance with the old A66 stretches only as far as its width, for on the other side a comprehensively embowered footpath leads unerringly to Crosthwaite church.

Crosthwaite Church and Skiddaw fells

Great Crosthwaite, more commonly referred to simply as Crosthwaite, is a tiny settlement becoming absorbed into Keswick. However it still maintains an independent air, with the river Greta forming a natural boundary. There is no central feature in Crosthwaite: a cosy inn stands near the bypass roundabout, while down the side road Lairthwaite School in its spacious grounds looks out across the north-western fells with the attractive parish church of St. Kentigern in the foreground.

There has been a church on this site since the 6th century, and parts of the present structure date back to the 12th century. Of particular interest are a collection of consecration crosses, an ancient font and the Radcliffe tomb. A plaque recalls Canon Rawnsley, co-founder of the National Trust and vicar here for 34 years. Here also is a splendid white marble memorial to the poet Southey, whose grave can be seen in the churchyard.

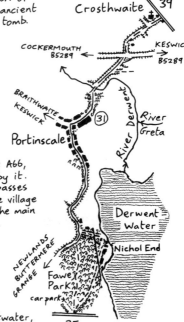

Portinscale stands on the other side of the A66, and long since avoided by it. Before the days of bypasses our own route out of the village would have been along the main road, for what is now a footbridge then carried the through traffic.

Portinscale's setting is an enviable one. It stands at the entrance to the Newlands valley and near the foot of Derwentwater, sufficiently distant from Keswick to maintain an air of tranquillity.

Keswick on Derwentwater

Dressed up in its Sunday name, Keswick is the undisputed capital of Northern Lakeland. From here roads radiate in all directions: to the lakes of Ullswater, Buttermere, Crummock Water and Bassenthwaite, while the main artery of Lakeland leads past Thirlmere to the southern half of the district. The lake that Keswick boasts as the best, however, is its own Derwentwater, which laps up to the edge of town. Dubbed 'Queen of the English Lakes', it forms a formidable trio with Keswick and Skiddaw, the northernmost 3000-footer which rises impressively behind town and lake.

The town itself stands on the banks of the river Greta, and its central feature is a sloping main street across which a host of shops and disappearing inns glare at each other. Only interruption is the historic Moot Hall, standing island-like in the centre and partly used as an information centre. A market was granted here over 700 years ago. Probably the most important building is Greta Hall, for 40 years home of Poet Laureate Robert Southey, where he played host to a procession of contemporaries including Wordsworth himself.

A claim to fame which will evoke many a childhood memory is the local pencil industry. Graphite from Borrowdale was first used four centuries ago, when Keswick had the world's first pencil factory. Still producing the goods — though in the care of a larger firm and without local ingredients — the Cumberland Pencil Company and its 'Lakeland' pencils will be long remembered. An interesting pencil museum is on the premises, while another museum on the road to the old station features a great model of Lakeland that took 17 years to create.

At one time the mid-point on the railway linking the fringe of Lakeland market towns of Cockermouth and Penrith, Keswick lost its last rail link in 1972, the section to Cockermouth having already disappeared in 1966. Roads have taken over here with a vengeance. The A66, joining the same two market towns, finally bypassed Keswick only a handful of years ago: now lorries bound for the west coast rumble under the foot of Skiddaw and on concrete bridges over the Greta, yet with little extra effort they could have bypassed the entire National Park by going only a few miles further north.

With tourism very much its major industry, Keswick caters for all visitors, even us.

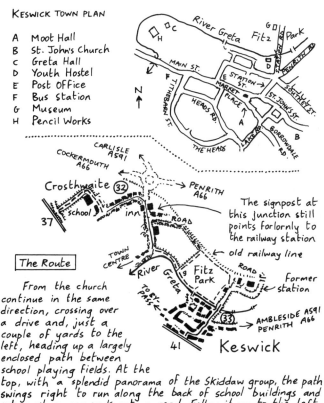

KESWICK TOWN PLAN

A Moot Hall
B St. John's Church
C Greta Hall
D Youth Hostel
E Post Office
F Bus Station
G Museum
H Pencil Works

The signpost at this junction still points forlornly to the railway station

old railway line

Former station

The Route

From the church continue in the same direction, crossing over a drive and, just a couple of yards to the left, heading up a largely enclosed path between school playing fields. At the top, with a splendid panorama of the Skiddaw group, the path swings right to run along the back of school buildings and out past a car park onto a road. Follow it up to the left between the varied architectural styles of Crosthwaite to join the A591 out of Keswick, only yards from the roundabout on the by-pass.

Turn right to the junction (Briar Rigg) just past the inn, then take either the enclosed parallel path off to the left, or continue past the hospital to a riverside path: both emerge into Fitz Park, which is crossed to join Station Road. Turn up it to cross river and main road into the town centre.

SECTION 4

——— KESWICK TO DOCKRAY ———

13 miles   2100 feet of ascent

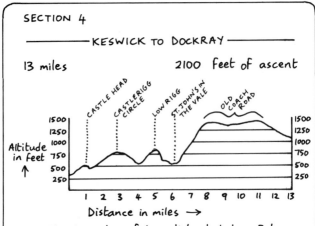

Altitude in feet ↑

Distance in miles →

This is a day of two distinct halves. Between Keswick and St. John's in the Vale the range of features include the rocky viewpoint of Castle Head, the dramatic setting of Castlerigg Stone Circle, and the colourful terrain of Low Rigg. From the fertile Vale of St. John, meanwhile, the route takes the Old Coach Road along the flanks of the Helvellyn range, to end the day above Ullswater.

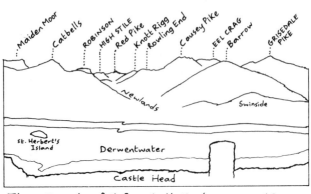

The north-western fells from Castle Head: see page 42

KESWICK to CASTLE HEAD

The Route

From the Moot Hall leave the Market Place by Lake Road, at its southern end. Passing the Dog and Gun the road twists along, and should be adhered to in order to gain a small roundabout on the edge of town. Continue across and along the Borrowdale road (path provided alongside). Within a quarter mile a gate on the left admits to Castlehead Wood, a National Trust sign confirming the location.

Climb the inviting path up to the left. Near the brow of the hill it swings right to gain the top of Castle Head, which is definitely not in doubt.

Keswick

the lake

BORROWDALE B5289

Castle Head (531')

39

43

The Moot Hall, Keswick

The Route

From the top of Castle Head retrace steps to the north and turn right to regain the path over the hill. It descends to a wicket gate before joining Springs Road: follow it to the right past the suburban dwellings to reach Springs Farm. The footpath hereabouts is copiously signposted, if not in the standard manner. Our path passes through a gate between the barns on the left, then climbs through the trees in the company of Brockle Beck. Soon it rises a little higher than the beck to provide far-reaching retrospective views.

In the higher reaches the pleasantest of paths crosses the temporarily subdued beck by means of a tiny wooden footbridge. Up the slope behind, a gate admits to the lane to Rakefoot, while a few yards to the left a stile is revealed on the right. From it follow the wall away to a stile in a fence, where a farm track is joined. Bear left along it, and remain on the track through several gates with attendant stiles to descend to the A591 Windermere–Keswick road. Cross straight over and along the narrow lane opposite. In a long half-mile access to the stone circle (which remains hidden until the last moment) is by a stile on the right.

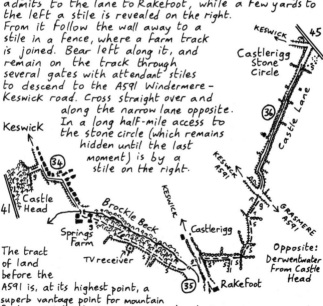

The tract of land before the A591 is, at its highest point, a superb vantage point for mountain features. The Helvellyn range, the shapely Grasmoor group, and both northern giants Skiddaw and Blencathra fill the scene.

43

The Route

Leave the stone circle by heading in the direction of Blencathra, to a gate which is the main entrance to the circle. Turn right along the road to descend past the farm of Goose Well, until a stile on the right admits to a large expanse of rough pasture. A sketchy path accompanies the fence down to a gate in the bottom wall. From it a stile by a gate gives access to the road about to cross Naddle Bridge. Turn right up this long defunct section of road to a junction with the old A66, itself bypassed many years ago by a modern 'improved' highway.

At the next junction turn off to the right on a lane which bends about sharply, but is soon left by a gate on the right. An old quarry track zigzags up the field, through a gate at the top and bears right past a former quarry. With Tewet Tarn just ahead the path fades: here bear left of the tarn to a stile in the wall ahead. A faint path heads away, past the head of the tarn to locate a stile in an intervening fence. Head up the slope of Low Rigg behind to arrive at a minor saddle on the gentle ridge. From a stile in the wall an inviting green path heads away through the bracken towards the Church of St John's in the Vale in its hause. A stile admits to the lane by the church: turn left along it.

Castlerigg and Blencathra

44

The ridge of Low Rigg is a good place to survey the route ahead, with the church, the Vale, Clough Head and the Old Coach Road all well displayed.

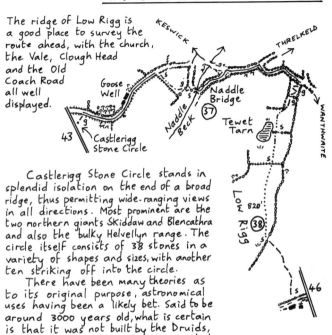

Castlerigg Stone Circle stands in splendid isolation on the end of a broad ridge, thus permitting wide-ranging views in all directions. Most prominent are the two northern giants Skiddaw and Blencathra and also the bulky Helvellyn range. The circle itself consists of 38 stones in a variety of shapes and sizes, with another ten striking off into the circle.

There have been many theories as to its original purpose, astronomical uses having been a likely bet. Said to be around 3000 years old, what is certain is that it was not built by the Druids, as has often been romantically suggested.

The Church of St. John's in the Vale fits snugly into the fellside between High Rigg and its neighbour Low Rigg. Dating only from the mid-19th century, it is attractively constructed of local materials. The interior is warm and welcoming, and clearly well maintained. Its situation on a low pass enables folk from either valley to reach it with equal ease. It boasts a 300 year old sundial. The adjacent school is now a youth centre.

The Route

The lane past the church soon begins a steep descent, but at its first swing left it is abandoned in favour of a small gate in the wall down to the right. A steep path through the bracken aims for the prominent buildings of Bridge House down below, a pair of simple footbridges assisting in the approach. Pass between the buildings and turn left along the drive, and at the first opportunity cross a narrow footbridge over St. John's Beck.

Turn left along the bank, over a stile and then along to a gate. Once through it leave the beckside and head away with a wall: the sketchy path heads straight across the field to a ladder stile in the facing wall. On the other side a farm track is joined and followed in the same direction to emerge onto the Thirlmere-Threlkeld road. Walk left for a couple of hundred yards then take the enclosed rough road on the right signposted to Matterdale.

After winding up, the track veers left away from the farm buildings of Wanthwaite to run below the old quarries to two adjacent gates. From the right one the Old Coach Road rises across another track before gradients ease for the long trek to Mariel Bridge.

Where the Coach Rd. leaves the quarries one can still see the line of a mineral railway that linked with quarries in both directions.

The Vale of St. John - otherwise St. John's in the Vale - is a pleasant green strath sandwiched between fells of widely contrasting stature. St. John's Beck meanders for five miles from the Thirlmere dam to join the river Greta.

At a height of 2847 ft Blencathra is one of the highest as well as shapeliest of Lakeland peaks, and we are very fortunate that it dominates the view for so much of the day.

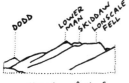

DODD LOWER MAN SKIDDAW LONSCALE FELL

Skiddaw fells from
the Old Coach Road

site of ancient
British settlement

The Old Coach Road is followed
throughout its length from St. John's
in the Vale to Dockray. It is a superbly
engineered route with good gradients,
drainage and surface. Apparently its
name is a little misleading, for it is
thought to have seen much use as a
peat road. It is hard to
imagine that even in
these enlightened days
someone could even
suggest laying
a full surface
over it.

Old Coach Road

The Clough
Head alternative
climbs through parallel
quarry tracks, zigzags
tidily up the fellside and
scrambles roughly
onto the summit
plateau.

41

Hause
Well   1450

summit
of road

White
Pike

48

From Clough Head's
summit the alternative
heads north-east to the outcrop
of White Pike, from where a choice
of grassy descents is available.

▲ CLOUGH
HEAD
2381'

The map has been extended to the south to
incorporate an energetic variation over the summit of
Clough Head, the northernmost outlier of the great
Helvellyn range. It demands an extra thousand feet
of ascent, and should only be attempted in the clearest
weather and when time is still on your side.

The Route

On arrival at the unassuming Mariel Bridge we have nevertheless reached an important stage of the day. Here, as Mosedale Beck is crossed, the domain of Clough Head is finally escaped and the far-reaching slopes of Great Dodd transport us through to Dockray. At a gate just beyond the bridge, the attendant fence at last comes to a halt and the track wanders free again. Wolfcrag Moss is conveniently avoided by taking in the gentle rise of Barbary Rigg, the track then returning to the foot of the slopes before rounding a major corner above the top of a Forestry Commission plantation.

With a fence for company again the track crosses Groove Beck to soon arrive at a crossroads with surfaced roads. This is High Row, and a signpost – which from further back appeared to rise in the middle of nowhere – points the route straight across towards Ullswater. The lane descends rapidly into Dockray.

47 42   Mosedale Beck

Mariel Bridge

9

Barbary Rigg   Fold

43

Wolfcrag Moss

Old Coach Road

Wolf Crags

slopes of Great Dodd

Swashbuckling Barbaryrigg Fold is a solid stone sheepfold which makes a pleasant foreground to the view of Blencathra, whose close companionship will soon be just a memory.

Wolf Crags from Mariel Bridge

Dockray

On arrival at High Row we reach an important stage of the walk. All previous water crossed has flowed into the Irish Sea by a variety of outlets, but Aira Beck and all further watercourses are destined for the Solway Firth by way of the river Eden.

Tiny Dockray displays nothing of exceptional architectural or historic interest, but also happily missing are the trappings of the modern age. Its life-blood is the main road leaving Ullswater for the A66, while the focal point is where the inn overlooks the bridge over Aira Beck. The 'bulk' of Dockrays extends westward, some attractive cottages lining the lane to High Row.

Old Coach Road

Groove Beck

44

Blake Sike

TROUTBECK

1352'

High Row

45

Aira Beck

Dockray

51

The vast expanse of fellside leading up to Great Dodd is generally known as Matterdale Common, designated a 'recreation area' for hang-gliding, ski-ing and – according to the sign- 'other'. To what can this refer?

Though rising in Deepdale and showing much character above Dockray, Aira Beck will always be known only for its antics downstream.

49

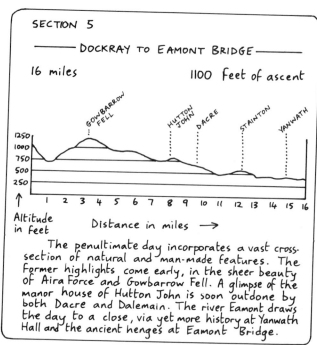

SECTION 5

——— DOCKRAY TO EAMONT BRIDGE ———

16 miles   1100 feet of ascent

The penultimate day incorporates a vast cross-section of natural and man-made features. The former highlights come early, in the sheer beauty of Aira Force and Gowbarrow Fell. A glimpse of the manor house of Hutton John is soon outdone by both Dacre and Dalemain. The river Eamont draws the day to a close, via yet more history at Yanwath Hall and the ancient henges at Eamont Bridge.

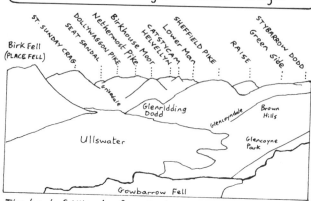

The head of Ullswater from Gowbarrow Fell: see page 54

The Route

Leave the main road through Dockray almost opposite the inn along a walled farm track. Beyond a gate it becomes unenclosed to wind down through a tract of rough pasture and renew our acquaintance with Aira Beck. Descending to the front of a farmhouse, our way continues as a footpath crossing tiny Riddings Beck and slanting up the field behind.

Beyond a gate the path heads downstream, with parallel Aira Beck now just below. At this point a first, memorable view of Ullswater is gained. Passing in and out of a wood the path continues down to the lovely environs of High Force. Just below it is a small footbridge, and from it either bank can be followed down to the stone-arched footbridge over the top of Aira Force.

The aim now is to gain the foot of the waterfall to savour the glory of the more traditional vantage point, and once again paths scramble down either side to the viewing bridge at the bottom. After the fascinating downward peer, this classic prospect puts the scale of the falls into proper perspective.

When the time comes to leave, take the wide lower path downstream (on the east, true left bank) to another bridge. Without crossing it, take the path up by the fence, across to a stile in a facing fence to meet a path on the open fell.

Conveniences and cafe (seasonal) five minutes away over the bridge

The dramatically sited upper bridge bears a tablet with a touching addition

Stephen Edward Spring Rice CB
1856 - 1902

He would have liked his brother Gerald, who 14 years after him also gave his life for his country, to be commemorated on this spot

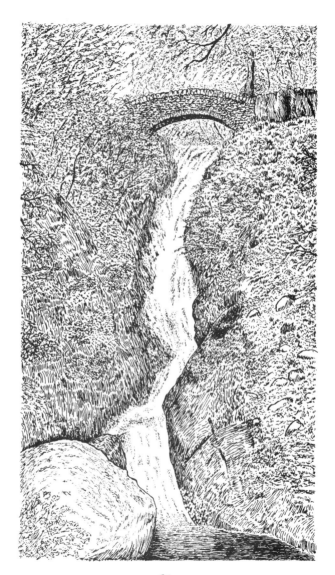

The Route

Turn right along the inviting path along the foot of Gowbarrow Fell, with shimmering Ullswater down to the right. At an early fork take the rather more strenuous – looking left branch. In practice it rises effortlessly across the breast of the fell, and soon eases out to permit all thoughts to be deployed on the view. A little further and a major vantage point is gained on a green knoll high above the outcrop of Yew Crag. Just across the fence is a substantial cairn deserving a visit.

Rounding the corner the path climbs a little further before meandering above steep slopes on Gowbarrow's eastern flank. Two first-class beck crossings are encountered – the latter having been sanitised by the addition of a wooden bridge – before arrival at a ruin, the remains of a shooting-box.

A wall and a fence are crossed by stiles in quick succession to enter the new plantations of Swinburn's Park. The path maintains its pleasant course around the lower slopes of Great Meldrum, though the bracken cover and extensive views are being elbowed out by the conifers.

Colourful Gowbarrow Fell reaches 1578 feet in height. The summit is located half a mile west of the shooting-box.

Opposite: Aira Force

Unusually shaped Lyulph's Tower is clearly visible from the path above. It was built as a shooting lodge where an old tower stood.

The Route

Our long-running footpath continues through the trees under the minor outcrops of Little Meldrum to arrive at a stile in a fence. From it continue on to where the fence meets a wall: a second stile takes the path to the left with the wall, and from a gate it descends towards the former rectory of Watermillock Church, which itself appears ahead. Swinging round to the left, the path passes above the rear of the house, past an old quarry to arrive at a wicket-gate onto a road almost opposite the former school.

All Saints, Watermillock is a beautiful church in a situation to match: from the churchyard one can gaze across Ullswater to the long line of fells on the opposite side of the lake. Built of local materials this sturdy church is merely a century old, replacing a 300 year old structure on the same spot. Though not boasting any spectacular features, both the interior and grounds are impeccably maintained.

Opposite: the head of Ullswater from the cairn above Yew Crag

Watermillock Church

55

The Route

Head left up the road and then right at the first junction. After passing Cove where the attractive farmhouse is subdued by its newer surroundings, look for a stile on the left. Rather hesitantly it leads into a young plantation, which fortunately is only a few trees deep. Bear diagonally right across this and the next two fields, guided by stiles. From the last stile bear left alongside the fence, and after another intervening gate aim straight for the buildings at Tongue ahead. Its confines are skirted by a track to the left, emerging via a gate onto the farm road to Mellfell House.

Cross straight over, and bearing a little to the right, negotiate stiles in two intervening fences to find yourself in what appears to be someone's back garden. Keeping left of the house at Land Ends, turn left to pass along the front of a row of wooden chalets. At their demise watch carefully for a small footpath sign pointing unconvincingly up the slope to the left. At the top turn right towards a stile by a gate.

Ahead now can be seen the next objective, the farm at Grovefoot. Aim directly for it, over another stile and along in the company of the fence on the left. A little before the farm we are treated to a permissive path to avoid its confines. This involves taking a stile in the fence to bypass the farmyard, whereupon a second stile returns us to the farm drive beyond the buildings. This is followed all the way out onto a quiet road: turn right, and after 250 yards a track branches off to the left to enter the farmstead of Lanehead.

Again keeping left of the buildings, take a gate just to the left of a large modern barn behind the farm. A path heads away bound on one side by a row of trees, and runs to a gate in the corner with a derelict farmhouse (now only a barn) behind. Pass round the front of it and head down the field to a stile in the fence at the bottom. Entering an extra-large field, bear half-right across it to locate a short-lived track where it crosses a tiny beck. Heading directly away from it a gate onto another lane is reached.

Turn left along this quiet road which descends to the attractive grouping at Sparket Mill. Ignore both the turn-off there, and the one to Hutton a short time after crossing Dacre Beck, and remain on the same road climbing past the grounds of Hutton John.

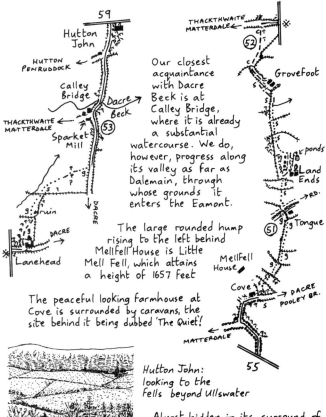

59

Hutton John

HUTTON PENRUDDOCK ←

Calley Bridge

Dacre Beck

THACKTHWAITE MATTERDALE ←

53

Sparket Mill

DACRE

? ? ruin

g

← DACRE

✳ Lanehead

THACKTHWAITE MATTERDALE ←

✳

52

Grovefoot

ponds

Land Ends

RD.

51

g Tongue

MellFell House

g

Cove

→ DACRE POOLEY BR.

MATTERDALE ↙

55

Our closest acquaintance with Dacre Beck is at Calley Bridge, where it is already a substantial watercourse. We do, however, progress along its valley as far as Dalemain, through whose grounds it enters the Eamont.

The large rounded hump rising to the left behind Mellfell House is Little Mell Fell, which attains a height of 1657 feet

The peaceful looking farmhouse at Cove is surrounded by caravans, the site behind it being dubbed 'The Quiet'!

Hutton John: looking to the fells beyond Ullswater

Almost hidden in its surround of fine gardens and woodland, Hutton John is a fortified manor house in the same family since Elizabethan times. The 600 year old tower was joined by various later additions, creating a mixture of architectural styles. Open by appointment only.

57

Considering its size, Dacre is not so much steeped in history as swamped in it. This tiny village nestles in its own hidden valley, and though inside the National Park it is well off the main tourist beat. Dacre boasts a church and a castle which both look down on many centuries from only a field apart.

Dacre Church

The church dates from Norman times, with an arch into the nave surviving from then. It is said to be the site of an old monastery, and also thought to have been the meeting place of King Athelstan of England and King Constantine of Scotland in 926. Inside the church, with its memorials to the Hasell family of Dalemain, can be found parts of ancient cross shafts, both Anglian and Viking.

In the churchyard are a unique quartet of carved stones, bears that guard each corner, with no two quite the same. From the bear occupying the south-east corner the castle is seen to good advantage. Its early 14th century walls are up to seven feet thick, and this former pele tower remains little changed, being well maintained as a private residence.

Dacre Castle

The Route

Continue up the road past Hutton John, to leave it by a stile on the right at a bend just after the trees end. Head straight across the field to a rather grand barn, much in keeping with the large house itself which can now be clearly seen just down to the right. Take a stile to the left of the barn, and head directly away in the company of a fence. This level course is maintained for some time.

Enjoying fine views across the valley of Dacre Beck, stiles take us over two intervening fences, and at the third a stile conveys us to the right side of the fence. Continuing on the level, the path soon becomes clear again in the shape of a farm track. Beyond another stile in a wall the track heads all the way to Dacrebank Farm, clearly visible ahead.

It should not be followed all the way to the farm, but vacated by a stile set into the wall on the right just before reaching a gateway to approach the farm. From the stile head over the brow of a field (keeping left of a barn) to locate a ladder stile in the wall opposite. From the stile-top Dacre's church tower and castle reveal themselves, helping to point the way.

Cross the large field in front to the wall at the far side, and continue down with it to reach a gate after a fence has taken over. Through the gate cross straight over the field to a stile just above the first house in Dacre. Turn right down the road to gain the centre of this quiet village.

59

The Route

After passing the unassuming Post Office on the left, take a broad drive off to the left opposite a 1953 Coronation seat. The castle itself and the muddy environs of a farm are met at close quarters before the track drops down to the bottom of the field. From there it becomes dead level, and can be followed at a cracking pace all the way to the stately house of Dalemain. The track runs into the courtyard at the rear of the house, which may well be thronged with visitors slurping ice cream. Pass under the archway just to the left to enter the car park, from where a drive leads out onto the Patterdale - Penrith road.

Turn left along the road for a short distance only, to leave it by an iron gate on the left opposite a house. Bear right up the field to a stile in the fence at the top. A pleasant path climbs through Evening Bank Wood, to negotiate some man-made steps through a gap in a low limestone scar. Leaving the wood by a stile in a fence, a fine stile in the wall to the right leads to the next field. Follow on to the left through a gateway and on into a tapering field corner. From the gate there cross to the far corner of the field, now on the very edge of Stainton.

A delightful grassy byway heads away from the gate, but is vacated almost at once by a stile on the left to join a drive. A right turn leads onto a lane, and turning down to the right it arrives at a crossroads in Stainton village.

Head straight across, and just past the end of the green turn off along a minor road to the right, just before a hotel. Within a minute leave this by a stile alongside a gate after the last building on the left. Head along to a second one and then down the field to the first of several characterful gapstiles. Cross a tiny stream and bear right, past a field corner to climb to a prominent gapstile above. Continue on past another wall corner to locate a stile to join a road. Only a few yards to the right turn down a peaceful enclosed track to the A592, and with care cross straight over.

Stainton is a spacious village, a cosmopolitan dormitory of Penrith. The date 1721 appears above the inn door, and attractive cottages line the triangular green, while much more 'up-market' housing spreads away from it. The pleasant open atmosphere is assisted by Stainton's position – though only two miles from Penrith it hides between the two main roads which radiate out to the west of the town.

Evening Bank Wood

Dalemain

Dacre Beck

River Eamont

Dalemain is a splendid country house in a rich parkland setting, making an impressive sight when viewed from the A592. An elegant Georgian facade hides architectural styles of many eras. It has been in the possession of the Hasell family for over 300 years, and was most likely in use as a more modest pele tower long before. It is open to the public during the main visitor season.

Dalemain: south front

The Route

From the A592 the grassy lane descends to the river Eamont. Do not go quite to the water's edge, instead locate a suspect stile in the left-hand wall. The Way now heads downstream on the riverbank, passing through a lovely section of woodland before a purely functional footbridge transports us to the opposite bank. A few yards further a stile is encountered, from where the Way climbs to follow the field edge above the wooded riverbank: an alternative path remains in the trees.

At the end of the field drop down to cross a tiny inflowing beck by a new little footbridge. Remaining near the river in this delightful little corner, a plank bridge is reached across a similar trickle, from where the path opts for the increasingly defined bank above the Eamont. After an intervening fence the river below turns through a well wooded bend, and here our higher route encounters three stiles in rapid succession.

Ahead now looms the impressive Yanwath Hall, with the busy railway line behind. From the stiles keep right to accompany a hedge along the length of an extensive pasture, turning left at the far end to reach a gate in the wall. Possibly after a closer glance at the hall down to the left, pass straight under the railway bridge. Tiny Yanwath is spread along to the right.

Yanwath Hall

Yanwath is a tiny settlement strung alongside the railway line on a dead-end road that leads to Yanwath's showpiece, the hall. This magnificent structure stands above the Eamont and dominates its surroundings. The striking feature is the battlemented pele tower which dates back over 650 years. Attached to this most solid edifice is the rest of the hall, set around a courtyard and itself over 300 years old. Looking very well maintained, it remains a working farm.

There are two further features of interest: immediately under the railway bridge is a large barn with slit windows, sheltering another attractive courtyard, while up the lane is an inn with mounting steps and two novel signs.

The railway line under which we pass is the main west coast line to Scotland, about to enter Penrith. This is one of the only two stations remaining on the whole stretch from Carnforth to Carlisle.

Yanwath Hall

Yanwath remainder of village under bridge

Sockbridge Mill

Stainton Island

We approach Yanwath on the Roman road to Brougham, fresh from its descent from the High Street mountain range.

At Yanwath

The river Eamont flows eleven miles from the outflow of Ullswater at Pooley Bridge to run into the Eden east of Penrith. It is therefore a full grown river from the outset, and during our journey we meet it on both sides of Eamont Bridge.

Throughout its course it forms the Cumberland-Westmorland boundary, and its two most historic bridges are crossed by the Way.

The Route

At the very base of the railway bridge an explicit direction sign points the way through a gate on the left. At once this private looking drive is vacated by means of an enticing but short-lived enclosed path on the right. On emerging into a field keep to its right side until a wall comes in from the left. Now switch allegiance to this left side, and keep on through a stile and a brace of wicket gates. Here the river is seen to be rejoined, forming a perfect U-bend between wooded banks far below. As the fence drops down towards the river, reality is restored by the sight of a caravan park and the M6 motorway. The edge of the former is skirted to reach the latter, with a wicket gate in the far corner leading to the cul de sac lane to the caravan site-cum-fish farm.

Turn right underneath the concrete bastions of the motorway, and up the gently rising lane. Just before the first house a stile on the left indicates the quickest way into Eamont Bridge, but a visit to Mayburgh should not be missed. Shortly after the last house a wicket gate gives access to the henge, which appears in striking fashion ahead. After an inspection return to the lane and a choice of routes into the village. The first continues up the lane to join another road into Eamont Bridge, allowing a visit to the less inspiring Round Table and perhaps more enticingly either of the hostelries. The second returns to the stile, crossing a field to join a drive running along to the bridge itself.

——— At Eamont Bridge ———

Mayburgh
looking to Cross Fell

In this Hive we are all Alive
Good Liquor makes us Funny
If you be dry step in and try
The Virtue of our HONEY

Inn sign

Eamont Bridge is yet another tiny village steeped in history that far outweighs its modest appearance. It takes its name, not unnaturally, from the fine sandstone bridge which has been the northern exit from the village for over 500 years, though widened to accommodate the A6. This highway, though since superceded by the M6 motorway, still carries a heavy volume of traffic, and as such, lights serve to ease the rumbling over the bridge.

Apart from a handful of cottages, Eamont Bridge stands proudly in Westmorland, and almost every building hugs the main road in customary fashion. A number of the cottages bear centuries-old datestones, and the two inns which face each other across the street can both look back on two and a half centuries. A feature at the adjacent B5320 junction is a memorial to two local men who died fighting in South Africa.

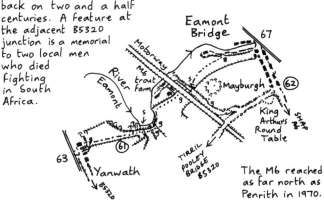

The M6 reached as far north as Penrith in 1970.

Eamont Bridge boasts two ancient earthworks, Mayburgh and King Arthur's Round Table. Thought to be around 4000 years old, the former is slightly the elder! It is also the most interesting: said to have been used as a place of worship, it is seen at its most dramatic on a dark, stormy day. The large circular mound is lined with trees and littered with rashes of stones. In the centre of what could be a little cricket pitch stands a lone monolith, 9 feet high and last remaining of several such stones. In contrast is the Round Table with its Arthurian legends obscured by time and its dried moat sliced into by the modern road on its northern side.

SECTION 6

—— EAMONT BRIDGE TO APPLEBY ——

18 miles   900 feet of ascent

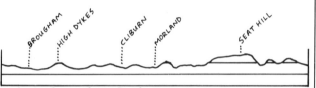

BROUGHAM
HIGH DYKES
CLIBURN
MORLAND
SEAT HILL

| 1 | 2 | 3 | 4 | 5 | 6 | 7 | 8 | 9 | 10 | 11 | 12 | 13 | 14 | 15 | 16 | 17 | 18 |

Altitude
in feet ↑   Distance in miles →

  With only an hour gone, we enter Westmorland
to conclude the walk, the Eamont being traced
to Brougham Castle. Quiet roads and waterside paths
lead to Cliburn and Morland, then the charms of
the river Lyvennet prove inspiring, particularly at
Jackdaw's Scar. More tracks and lanes lead to
Seat Hill, and with the long line of the Pennines
getting ever nearer, a bee-line march for Appleby
concludes in the company of the river Eden.

Boroughgate, Appleby

66

The Route

At the Penrith (north) end of the village, cross the footbridge next to the old bridge (a good deal safer for pedestrians) over the Eamont and immediately turn right along a drive towards a private house. Just before it take stiles left and quickly right into the trees. At once a path bears off to the right to leave an enclosed track, and runs through the wood at the rear of the house.

The path runs along to a stile to emerge onto the riverbank adjacent to a dodgy-looking footbridge. Happily it need not be tested, as the route simply clings to the riverbank around a mighty loop, taking in a brace of intervening stiles along the way. On reaching a swimming club turn sharply left to a stile in the hedge. Behind is a by-road that was once the A66. Turn right to its imminent junction with the modern road, and keep straight on the old way to the old bridge.

Home of the Carletons for 500 years, the hall is now a police HQ.

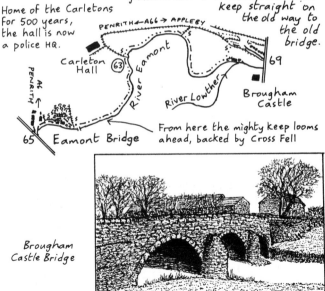

PENRITH ← A66 → APPLEBY

Carleton Hall

(63)

River Eamont

River Lowther

69

Brougham Castle

A6 PENRITH ↑

65   Eamont Bridge

From here the mighty keep looms ahead, backed by Cross Fell

Brougham Castle Bridge

At Brougham, history abounds: a ruined castle, the site of a Roman fort, and an old bridge over the Eamont combine well. The imposing remains of Brougham Castle preside over the confluence of the rivers Eamont and Lowther in an attractive rural setting. The oldest part is the Keep, dating from the late 12th century. In the possession of the Clifford family many extensions were added, and when it had been severely damaged in the Civil War, who else but the indomitable Lady Anne Clifford set about its restoration. The tomb of this great benefactress can be seen at the end of the day in Appleby, scene of more of her good deeds. Soon after her death Brougham fell into disrepair, and is now cared for by those modern day heroes, English Heritage.

The outline of the Roman fort can clearly be identified between the castle and the crossroads south of it. 'Brocavum', as it was known, was built by Agricola in a strategic position guarding the Ribchester to Carlisle road at its crossing of the Eamont. Sections of the fort were probably later put to good use as part of the castle's defences. The substantial sandstone bridge now stands in peace alongside the castle, mercifully bypassed by the A66.

Brougham
Castle

68

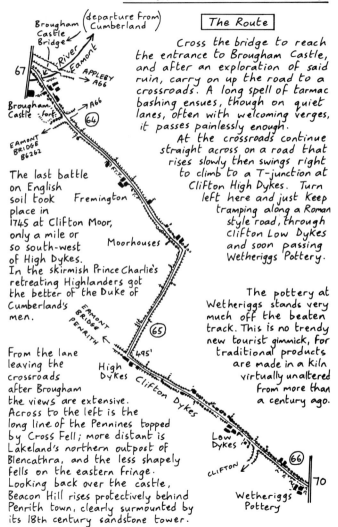

Brougham Castle Bridge

(departure from) Cumberland

River Eamont

APPLEBY A66

67

Brougham Castle fork

A66

64

EAMONT BRIDGE B6262

Fremington

Moorhouses

EAMONT BRIDGE PENRITH

65

495'

High Dykes

Clifton Dykes

Low Dykes

66

70

CLIFTON

Wetheriggs Pottery

The last battle on English soil took place in 1745 at Clifton Moor, only a mile or so south-west of High Dykes. In the skirmish Prince Charlie's retreating Highlanders got the better of the Duke of Cumberland's men.

From the lane leaving the crossroads after Brougham the views are extensive. Across to the left is the long line of the Pennines topped by Cross Fell; more distant is Lakeland's northern outpost of Blencathra, and the less shapely fells on the eastern fringe. Looking back over the castle, Beacon Hill rises protectively behind Penrith town, clearly surmounted by its 18th century sandstone tower.

| The Route |

Cross the bridge to reach the entrance to Brougham Castle, and after an exploration of said ruin, carry on up the road to a crossroads. A long spell of tarmac bashing ensues, though on quiet lanes, often with welcoming verges, it passes painlessly enough.

At the crossroads continue straight across on a road that rises slowly then swings right to climb to a T-junction at Clifton High Dykes. Turn left here and just keep tramping along a Roman style road, through Clifton Low Dykes and soon passing Wetheriggs Pottery.

The pottery at Wetheriggs stands very much off the beaten track. This is no trendy new tourist gimmick, for traditional products are made in a kiln virtually unaltered from more than a century ago.

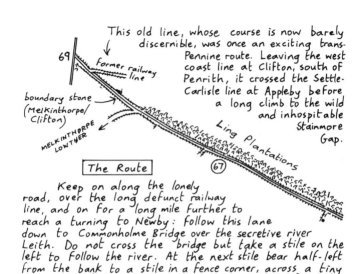

This old line, whose course is now barely discernible, was once an exciting trans-Pennine route. Leaving the west coast line at Clifton, south of Penrith, it crossed the Settle-Carlisle line at Appleby before a long climb to the wild and inhospitable Stainmore Gap.

69

former railway line

boundary stone (Melkinthorpe/ Clifton)

MELKINTHORPE LOWTHER

Ling Plantations

The Route

67

Keep on along the lonely road, over the long defunct railway line, and on for a long mile further to reach a turning to Newby: follow this lane down to Commonholme Bridge over the secretive river Leith. Do not cross the bridge but take a stile on the left to follow the river. At the next stile bear half-left from the bank to a stile in a fence corner, across a tiny 'syke'. Now follow the fence right, below a bank of scrub. When the fence turns right keep on to a lone gate-post, then bear up the slope to the left. Without joining the drive to Leith House, swing down to the right again to use a gate in the fence running down the hill.

A thin path heads away from the gate, hugging the foot of the sandstone slope. From a stile in an intervening fence Cliburn appears ahead, and aiming for the village a muddy farm track will be reached climbing from the far end of the riverside pasture. It enters the labyrinthian complex of traditional and modern farm buildings of Rectory Farm, and a swift left-right-left between them will lead out onto the road through the village.

Although the bulk of Cliburn is up to the left, the Way turns down to cross the Leith by means of Cliburn Town Bridge. Immediately across, take the drive heading off to the left from a cattle grid. Before it reaches the house turn off up the field to a gate in the far corner. From it head straight up the fieldside, past a minor kink in the fence to another top-corner gate. Here a track is joined to run along to the environs of Akeygate and out on its drive to join a road.

Go straight ahead for about 200 yards, then turn down the first metalled track on the left.

Cliburn is another of the many tiny villages which cling tightly to a single road, with little, if any, other development. From a crossroads where stands the inn, a lane slopes steadily down to the church, which itself stands high above the river Leith. The charm of St. Cuthberts is its simplicity: better appreciated from the river than the road (where trees hide it) its sandstone walls contain much history. Of special note are a Norman chancel arch, and set in the porch walls, two inscribed Roman stones.

Across the road, in a farming setting, is the hall which incorporates a medieval defensive tower.

Of great surprise at Commonholme Bridge is a sandstone outcrop so out of place in its rural surround.

The boundary stone

→ CLIBURN BOLTON

68 Commonholme Bridge

Leith House

→ BOLTON

Cliburn

Hall

69

GT. STRICKLAND NEWBY

River Leith

In its ten mile journey the Leith makes a good job of avoiding civilisation

Cliburn Town Bridge

ROAD

across: Cliburn Church

Akeygate

73

MORLAND

The Route

When the narrow lane divides into three, opt for the right branch, and leave it by the second stile on the right just before the first cottage. Head down the fieldside, over two intervening stiles to reach *Morland Beck* in the serene environs of *Glenton Vale*. Pass through a gate to use the narrow footbridge over the beck, then accompany its grassy bank upstream. In this park-like setting it leads unerringly towards Morland village.

A tiny footbridge is reached in a charming location at the edge of the village: cross it to leave this idyllic spot by the snicket to the right. It debouches onto the road by the church, but a more interesting exercise is to take the short-cut into the churchyard on the left. An almost hidden pathway sneaks out of the south-east corner to empty into the centre of Morland.

Turn down the short way to an inn, then right alongside it and on past a second inn. Cross yet another little footbridge and head up the lane behind. It soon joins another lane out of the village to continue a short, steep climb. At the brow of the hill take the farm drive on the right, and follow it to its demise at *Kemplee*.

Deflect round to the right of the buildings to descend by an orchard to cross *Chapel Bridge* over the river *Lyvennet*. Turn immediately right along an indistinct path which clings to the river, passing in and out of a wood as it goes.

Morland Church

72

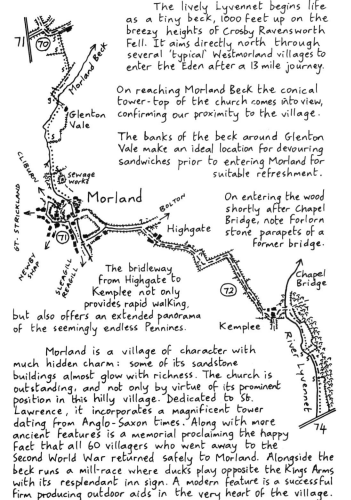

The lively Lyvennet begins life as a tiny beck, 1000 feet up on the breezy heights of Crosby Ravensworth Fell. It aims directly north through several 'typical' Westmorland villages to enter the Eden after a 13 mile journey.

On reaching Morland Beck the conical tower-top of the church comes into view, confirming our proximity to the village.

The banks of the beck around Glenton Vale make an ideal location for devouring sandwiches prior to entering Morland for suitable refreshment.

On entering the wood shortly after Chapel Bridge, note forlorn stone parapets of a former bridge.

The bridleway from Highgate to Kemplee not only provides rapid walking, but also offers an extended panorama of the seemingly endless Pennines.

Morland is a village of character with much hidden charm: some of its sandstone buildings almost glow with richness. The church is outstanding, and not only by virtue of its prominent position in this hilly village. Dedicated to St. Lawrence, it incorporates a magnificent tower dating from Anglo-Saxon times. Along with more ancient features is a memorial proclaiming the happy fact that all 60 villagers who went away to the Second World War returned safely to Morland. Alongside the beck runs a mill-race where ducks play opposite the Kings Arms with its resplendant inn sign. A modern feature is a successful firm producing outdoor aids in the very heart of the village.

King's Meaburn is only a minute's walk up the steep lane from the ford, its few houses and farms spread along a minor road. Definitely a backwater, its tiny school only recently closed its doors for the last time. An inn remains to offer its own particular social value in this rural quarter.

Should lack of time become a problem note that the road via King's Meaburn and/or the lane to Colby will save some. The route would then be rejoined at the end of page 77, just out of Appleby.

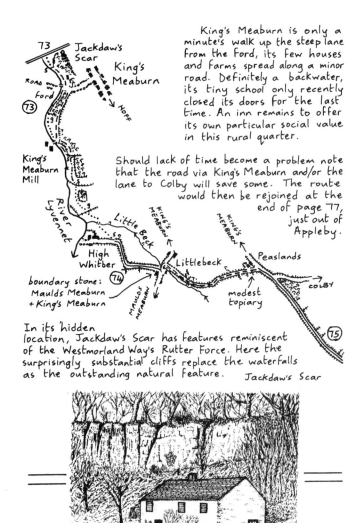

73 Jackdaw's Scar

King's Meaburn

ROAD

ford

73

HOFF

King's Meaburn Mill

River Lyvennet

Little Beck

KING'S MEABURN

KING'S MEABURN

KING'S MEABURN

High Whitber

boundary stone: Maulds Meaburn + King's Meaburn

74

MAULDS MEABURN

Littlebeck

Peaslands

modest topiary

COLBY

75

In its hidden location, Jackdaw's Scar has features reminiscent of the Westmorland Way's Rutter Force. Here the surprisingly substantial cliffs replace the waterfalls as the outstanding natural feature. Jackdaw's Scar

The Route

Remaining with the river, the Way reaches a stile from where a track runs along the front of a lone cottage and out onto a lane. In this delightful setting embowered in trees, the Lyvennet is crossed by a ford and spanned by a long, narrow footbridge: the cliffs of Jackdaw's Scar climb high above the cottage.

Across the lane a path runs through the trees, soon emerging into a riverside pasture. The driveway to King's Meaburn Mill is joined before it crosses the river. Do not cross, but instead locate a hurdle at the start of the bridge, dropping down some steps to the river. From here the path climbs a little in the trees above a rough bank, fighting its way through to a stile to drop back down to a pasture. Keeping below enclosed plantations, a stile and then a gate is reached, with the farm of High Whitber ahead. Bear left to cross meandering Little Beck by a rickety bridge, and maintain that direction to find a stile by a lone tree and a greenhouse. Emerging onto a narrow road, turn away from the farm and go left to a junction at Littlebeck.

Go left the few yards over the bridge, then head right up a green lane to climb to a high road which parallels the Lyvennet for some miles. On turning right, this final road section is a quiet, level mile and three-quarters. The point of departure is unmistakable, being directly opposite the lane branching down to Maulds Meaburn.

The remaining miles to Appleby form virtually a bee-line: a good track sets off in forthright mood across expanses of rough pasture.

Half a mile down the lane to Maulds Meaburn is the large house of Holesfoot, open to the public as an ancestral research centre.

The boundary stone is another inscribed with the initials of both the Meaburn villages

boundary stone

77

76

656'

Seat Hill

MAULDS MEABURN

HOFF

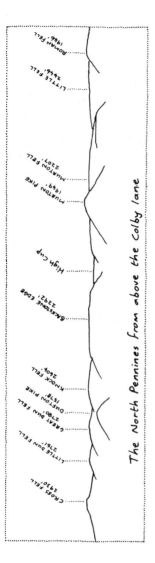

The North Pennines from above the Colby lane

ROMAN FELL 1966'
LITTLE FELL 2446'
MURTON FELL 2207'
MURTON PIKE 1949'
High Cup
BACKSTONE EDGE 2292'
KNOCK FELL 2604'
DUFTON PIKE 1578'
GREAT DUN FELL 2780'
LITTLE DUN FELL 2761'
CROSS FELL 2930'

Maintaining the same line, the track fades away before reaching a gate in the corner overshadowed by trees. From here on trees are very much in evidence, and with a fence on the left a clearer path heads for a stile. From it it heads off through the trees again to descend to the trickle of Nether Hoff Syke.

A little grassed stone-arch bridge transports us to a stile opposite, from where a rise is topped before dropping down to another gate and more woodland. Once again clear, a track leads past the local sheep's dining area to fall to Hoff Beck: on leaving the trees swing left along a green strath to the metal Bandley Bridge.

An obvious path ascends the opposite slope, various hedges and undergrowth on either side tunnelling our path through a gate. This long-established pathway climbs the hillside, its enclosure on the left now limited to a few loose trees and bushes.

Shortly after a gateway the way breaks out of its confined channel as a pair of white marker posts guide it into a field. Follow the side away, turning left at the corner to locate an iron stile by a gate hiding a hedge-bound green lane. This runs along to a road, which is crossed straight over and up an uninspiring suburban road.

On turning the page
and leaving the
modern housing, the
river Eden comes
into view. Sadly it
isn't encountered until
the last mile of the
walk, so make the
most of its company.
Though wholly
Cumbrian, the Eden

Bandley Bridge

springs forth only a mile from the
Yorkshire border on the high fells of
lonely Mallerstang, to flow northward
through an ever widening and ever more
fertile vale before eventually entering the
Solway Firth beyond Carlisle. Ensure that
acquaintance with it is soon made stronger.

On topping the last rise one can clearly
glimpse through the trees the impressive
Keep of Appleby Castle.
Nearly there now!

Hoff Beck flows northward like
the Eden, covering some attractive
wooded miles before its demise.
The hamlet of Hoff is a mile
upstream of Bandley
Bridge.
          It can be
rather muddy in here

The entire
route from the
lane above Maulds
Meaburn to the lane
to Colby is designated on
the Ordnance Survey maps
          as a bridlepath, and its switchback
          course is easy enough to follow. However
its value to horse-riders must be rendered a little more than
difficult by virtue of the ladder-stile and footbridge that are
met. Even to us the stile is a struggle at this late stage!

77

Appleby in Westmorland

Appleby is a classic country town, full of interest both ancient and modern. Until local government reorganisation Appleby proudly held the title of County Town of Westmorland, an honour bestowed on it long ago when it ranked of greater importance than Kendal. Indeed, Appleby seemed justified in its claim to have been England's smallest county town. When the old county disappeared and took Appleby's status with it, the town admirably decided on a name change to Appleby in Westmorland in order to preserve that particular link with the past.

It is very much the past that is in evidence here, for Appleby is steeped in history. The 'piece de resistance' must be the main street, known as Boroughgate, which extends from the parish church to the castle, rising gradually throughout. It is exceptionally broad, and lined with beautiful trees and an interesting assortment of buildings. The castle does not dominate the town despite its rightful position at the top of the hill, in fact it remains rather aloof. Best preserved portion is the Keep, while the grounds are open to visitors as one of the centres of the Rare Breeds Survival Trust.

The parish church dates from 1176 and is dedicated to St. Lawrence. This too is a little hidden, on this occasion by the cloisters built of the same sandstone, conveying the impression that the two are connected. The Eden makes a charming foreground to the church when viewed from the Sands, on its east bank. Turning away up Bongate is an old part of the town, formerly a parish in its own right: the church of St. Michael is no longer used as such, but is a splendid old structure.

Any mention of Appleby's history must include reference to Lady Anne Clifford, who performed a host of charitable deeds here : the restoration of St. Lawrence's in 1655, complete rebuilding of Bongate church, and in 1653 the building of some almshouses. After first-class restoration work, the latter are inhabited again, and can be seen well up Boroughgate. The castle itself was one of her many North-country possessions, and her tomb can be seen in the parish church, beneath a colourful marble display of her family's heraldic descent. Alongside is her mother's tomb, surmounted by a fine carved figure.

COLBY LANE to APPLEBY

The Route

From Barrowmoor Road twist a little right and head down Margaret's Way. At the bend a pathway between houses leads to a terrace high above a wooded bend of the river Eden. Follow it to the right to soon drop down into a quiet corner of Appleby.

Although a right turn will lead into the Market Place, the more fitting finale is to turn left along Holme Street and over a farm bridge: turn right then to accompany the Eden round another sharp curve to emerge onto the Sands. Recross the river by the main bridge to enter the Market Place in front of the Cloisters and the church.

Each year in early June, Appleby Horse Fair takes over the town. Hordes of horse-traders and travellers descend on the area to take part in a historic and colourful event lasting for several days.

THE FINISH

Appleby

PENRITH (A66)

River Eden

BROUGH (A66)

ORTON B6260

Castle

77

79

Appleby:
The Market Place

79

RECORD OF INNS VISITED

Inn	Location	Comments

....

THE COUNTRY CODE

Respect the life and work of the countryside
Protect wildlife, plants and trees
Keep to public paths across farmland
Safeguard water supplies
Go carefully on country roads
Keep dogs under control
Guard against all risks of fire
Fasten all gates
Leave no litter- take it with you
Make no unnecessary noise
Leave livestock, crops and machinery alone
Use gates and stiles to cross fences, hedges and walls

RECORD OF ACCOMMODATION

Date	Address	Comments

RECORD OF THE JOURNEY

Date	Place	Miles daily	Miles total	Times arrive	Times depart	Comments
	Ravenglass	–	–			
	Muncaster Mill	1¾	1¾			
	Irton Church	4	4			
	Santon Bridge	6	6			
	Nether Wasdale	9½	9½			
	Wasdale Hall	2¼	11¾			
	Wasdale Head	6½	16			
	Black Sail Hut	9½	19			
	Buttermere	13½	23			
	Rigg Pass	3	26			
	Rigg Beck	4¾	27¾			
	Skelgill	5¾	28¾			
	Portinscale	8	31			
	Crosthwaite Church	8½	31½			
	Keswick	10¼	33¼			
	Castle Head	½	33¾			
	Castlerigg Stone Circle	3	36¼			
	St. John's in the Vale Church	5	38¼			

Date	Place	Miles daily	Miles total	Times arrive	Times depart	Comments
	Wanthwaite	6	39¼			
	Mariel Bridge	8¾	42			
	High Row	11½	44¾			
	Dockray	12¾	46			
	Aira Force	¾	46¾			
	Watermillock Church	4	50			
	Sparket Mill	7	53			
	Dacre	9½	55½			
	Dalemain	11	57			
	Stainton	12¼	58¼			
	Yanwath	14¾	60¾			
	Eamont Bridge	16	62			
	Brougham Castle	1¾	63¾			
	Wetheriggs Pottery	4	66			
	Commonholme Bridge	6	68			
	Cliburn	7	69			
	Morland	9	71			
	Jackdaw's Scar	10¾	72¾			
	Littlebeck	12¼	74½			
	Seat Hill	14¼	76¼			
	Appleby	18	80			

THE WESTMORLAND WAY

POOLEY BRIDGE

Ullswater

APPLEBY

PATTERDALE

SHAP

GRASMERE

TROUTBECK

Windermere

Dove Cottage

KENDAL

Commencing under the Pennines this combines two unspoilt areas of rural Westmorland with the mountains and lakes of central Lakeland

98 miles from Appleby to Arnside

Morecambe Bay

ARNSIDE

ISBN 0 9509212 5 4
96 pages

Helvellyn group from Fairfield

THE DALES WAY

84 miles from
Ilkley to Bowness

*Through the heart
of the Yorkshire
Dales to the
Lake District*

Howgill Fells, Sedbergh   88 pages ISBN 1 870141 09 1

THE CLEVELAND WAY

109 miles from Helmsley
to Filey Brigg

*Moorland and coastal walking
around the North York Moors*

96 pages
ISBN 1 870141 17 2

Sutton Bank

THE COAST TO COAST WALK

190 miles from St. Bees
to Robin Hood's Bay

*The classic trek across
3 National Parks*

152 pages
ISBN 1 870141 18 0

Eagle Crag, Stonethwaite

INDEX OF PLACE-NAMES ON THE ROUTE-MAPS

ADDACOMB BECK — 31
AIRA BECK — 49,51
AIRA FORCE — 51
AKEYGATE — 71
APPLEBY — 79
ARD CRAGS — 32

BANDLEY BRIDGE — 77
BANDLEY WOOD — 77
BARBARY RIGG — 48
BIRKRIGG OAKS — 32
BIRKS WOOD — 19
BLACK SAIL HUT — 27
BLACK SAIL PASS — 25
BLAKE SIKE — 49
BOWDERDALE — 23
BRIDGE HOUSE — 46
BROCKLE BECK — 43
BROUGHAM CASTLE — 67,69
BROUGHAM CASTLE BRIDGE — 69
BURTNESS WOOD — 29
BUTTERMERE (lake) — 29
BUTTERMERE (village) — 29,31
BUTTERMERE DUBS — 29

CALLEY BRIDGE — 57
CASTLE HEAD — 41,43
CASTLE LANE — 43
CASTLERIGG — 43
CASTLERIGG STONE CIRCLE — 43,45
CAUSEY PIKE — 33
CHAPEL BRIDGE — 73
CINDERDALE BRIDGE — 21
CLIBURN — 71
CLIBURN TOWN BRIDGE — 71
CLIFTON DYKES — 69
CLOUGH HEAD — 47
COMB BECK — 29
COMMONHOLME BRIDGE — 71

COVE — 57
CRAGHOUSE BRIDGE — 19
CROSTHWAITE — 37,39

DACRE — 59
DACREBANK — 59
DACRE BECK — 57,60,61
DALEMAIN — 61
DERWENT, RIVER — 37
DERWENTWATER — 35,37
DOCKRAY — 49,51
DOWN IN THE DALE — 23

EAMONT BRIDGE — 65,67
EAMONT, RIVER — 61,63,65,67,69
EASTHWAITE — 21
EDEN, RIVER — 79
ENNERDALE FOREST — 27
ESK, RIVER — 15
EVENING BANK WOOD — 61

FAWE PARK — 37
FOREST BRIDGE — 21
FOX BIELD WOOD — 19
FREMINGTON — 69

GASKETH — 17
GATHERSTONE BECK — 25
GHYLL BANK — 35
GLENTON VALE — 73
GOOSE WELL — 45
GOWBARROW FELL — 53
GREAT DODD — 48
GREAT MELDRUM — 53
GRETA, RIVER — 37,39
GROOVE BECK — 49
GROVEFOOT — 57

HAUSE WELL	47	LEITH, RIVER	71
HAWSE END	35	LINGHOLM	35
HAYSTACKS	27	LINGMELL BECK	23
HIGH CRAG	29	LING PLANTATIONS	70
HIGH DYKES	69	LITTLEBECK	74
HIGH FORCE	51	LITTLE BECK	74
HIGHGATE	73	LITTLE MELDRUM	55
HIGH ROW	49	LIZA, RIVER	27
HIGH STILE	29	LOW DYKES	69
HIGH WHITBER	74	LOW RIGG	45
HILLTOP QUARRIES	46	LOWTHER, RIVER	67
HOFF BECK	77	LOW WOOD	21
HOLLINS	19	LUND BRIDGE	21
HOLLINS BRIDGE	19	LYULPH'S TOWER	53
HUTTON JOHN	57,59	LYVENNET, RIVER	73,74
IRTON CHURCH	17	MARIEL BRIDGE	48
IRTON HALL	17	MAYBURGH	65
IRT, RIVER	15,17,19,21	MELLFELL HOUSE	57
		MIDDLE FELL	23
		MITE, RIVER	15
JACKDAW'S SCAR	74	MOORGATE	17
		MOORHOUSES	69
		MORLAND	73
KEMPLEE	73	MORLAND BECK	73
KESWICK	39,41,43	MOSEDALE BECK, Coach Road	48
KING ARTHUR'S ROUND TABLE	65	MOSEDALE BECK, Wasdale	23,25
KING'S MEABURN	74	MUNCASTER MILL	15
KING'S MEABURN MILL	74	MUNCASTER PARK	15
KIRK FELL	25		
KIRKFELL CRAGS	25		
KIRKSTYLE GILL	53	NADDLE BECK	45
KNOTT RIGG	31	NADDLE BRIDGE	45
		NETHER BECK	23
		NETHERBECK BRIDGE	23
LAND ENDS	57	NETHERHOFF SIKE	77
LANEHEAD	57	NETHER WASDALE	19,21
LEITH HOUSE	71	NEWLANDS BECK	33,35
		NICHOL END	37

OLD COACH ROAD	46,47,48,49
OVER BECK	23
OVERBECK BRIDGE	23
PEASLANDS	74
PORTINSCALE	37
PRIEST'S CRAG	55
RAKEFOOT	43
RAVENGLASS	15
RAVENGLASS + ESKDALE RLY.	15
RIGG BECK	32,33
RIGG PASS	32
RIVER DERWENT	37
RIVER EAMONT	61,63,65,67,69
RIVER EDEN	79
RIVER ESK	15
RIVER GRETA	37,39
RIVER IRT	15,17,19,21
RIVER LEITH	71
RIVER LIZA	27
RIVER LOWTHER	67
RIVER LYVENNET	73,74
RIVER MITE	15
ROWLING END	33
ROWLING END (farm)	33
SAIL	32
SAIL BECK, Buttermere	31,32
SAIL BECK, Ennerdale	27
ST. JOHN'S BECK	46
ST. JOHN'S IN THE VALE	46
SANTON BRIDGE	17,19
SCAR CRAGS	32
SCARTH GAP	27
SEAT	27

SEAT HILL	75
SKELGILL	35
SOCKBRIDGE MILL	63
SOUR MILK GILL	29
SPARKET MILL	57
SPRINGS FARM	43
STAINTON	61
STAINTON ISLAND	63
STANGENDS	19
STANGENDS BRIDGE	19
SWINBURN'S PARK	53
TEWET TARN	45
THIRD GILL	31
TONGUE	57
WALLS CASTLE	15
WALLS MANSION	15
WALLS PLANTATION	15
WANDOPE	31
WANTHWAITE	46
WARNSCALE BECK	29
WASDALE HALL	21
WASDALE HEAD	23,25
WASTWATER	21,23
WATERMILLOCK CHURCH	55
WETHERIGGS POTTERY	69
WHITELESS PIKE	31
WHITE PIKE	47
WOLFCRAG MOSS	48
WOLF CRAGS	48
YANWATH	63,65
YANWATH HALL	63
YEWBARROW	23
YEW CRAG	53